Dice Activities for Multiplication

Facts • Fluency • Fun

Chet Delani, Mary Saltus, Diane Neison, Marcia Fitzgerald, Karen Moore

Order Number 210907
ISBN 978-1-58324-310-7

E F G H I 15 14 13 12 11

395 Main Street
Rowley, MA 01969
www.didax.com

Foreword

Classroom practice and research have overwhelmingly acknowledged that children learn most effectively through play. It is in the context of play that they willingly learn complicated rules, strategies, and maneuvers.

It is critical that children learn basic arithmetic facts, but classroom methods used today most commonly emphasize drills and worksheets that do not engage or motivate children. Often, students are required to "practice" the same drills for excessively long periods without any long-lasting results. Unfortunately, their vision of mathematics is through the lens of boring and tedious exercises. Perhaps even more frustrating, their learning potential in mathematics may be stunted and limited.

Students who experience challenging mathematical programs develop a profound curiosity about numerical, algebraic, and geometrical relationships and pursue their curiosity with purpose and engagement. With a solid handle on the basic mathematics facts, they can more easily navigate their way through more complex study in this exciting area. The activities in *Dice Activities for Multiplication* will work with any commercial program, and the teacher should witness how students willingly learn their facts in order to play the mathematical games presented.

The activities in this book focus on the NCTM content standard of number and operations. They also address the standards of reasoning, problem solving, and probability. The activities require only the use of dice, a commonly available manipulative.

Our work is continually expanding, and we welcome any suggestions for modification of these activities that will lead to improved mathematical thinking on the part of students.

—The authors, www.mathofcourse.com

Contents

Dice Activities for Multiplication Facts is designed for teachers and parents to use with children in grades 3–5. These engaging, challenging, and fun activities give students a variety of opportunities to practice multiplication facts without tedious paper-and-pencil drills.

Dice Activities for Multiplication Facts provides opportunities to:

- Develop fluency with multiplication facts 2 through 12
- Reinforce number patterns
- Recognize the commutative property of multiplication—for, example: $2 \times 8 = 8 \times 2$
- Develop game strategy
- Investigate the probability concept of chance
- Develop communication and cooperation skills by working in teams of two students

Dice Activities for Multiplication Facts presents seven dice activities for each of the multiplication number facts 2 through 12. All seven activities involve tossing two dice, finding the sum, and multiplying the sum by a number 2 through 12.

The Sum Dice Graph activities introduce the table of facts for a specific multiplication family of facts. Students toss two dice, find the sum of the two dice, and multiply the sum by the specified multiplicand for the activity. Students find the product on the graph. They either write the multiplication sentence (for example, 4×7) in the box above the product or they write the product itself in the box above the product. The multiples listed in sequence on the graph aid students in computing.

The Table Completion activities challenge students to fill in their chart before their opponent. The players are dependent on tossing sums between 2 and 12 before their opponent does. Some of the Table Completion activities involve students working on a different multiple than their opponent.

Three chart activities—Four in a Row, Square Off, and Cross Over—present a choice of activities involving strategies of placing four tokens in a row, forming a square with four tokens, or placing tokens so they cross the chart either vertically or horizontally.

The simple Tic-Tac-Toe activity is a game of chance. The players are more dependent on the toss of the dice than in any of the other activities. Not all possible multiples of 2 through 12 are represented. This activity is an introduction to the Four-Grid Tic-Tac-Toe activity.

Four-Grid Tic-Tac-Toe is less an activity of chance and more of a skill than simple Tic-Tac-Toe. Players place three tokens in a row on as many of the grids as they can until all possible moves have been played. Players then count their sets of three tokens in a row to determine who has the most. Players sometimes have a choice of blocking an opponent.

Assigning the same dice activity but different multiplication facts for specific students provides teachers with opportunities to differentiate class instruction and homework assignments.

Meeting the NCTM Standards

NCTM STANDARDS	Sum Dice Graph Activities Pages 1–14	Table Completion Chart Activities Pages 15–36	Four in a Row Activities Pages 37–49	Square Off Activities Pages 51–63	Cross Over Activities Pages 65–77	Tic-Tac-Toe Activities Pages 79–103
Number and Operations						
Place value						
Equivalent representations						
Fractions	X					
Addition and subtraction	X	X	X	X	X	X
Multiplication and division	X	X	X	X	X	X
Relationships between operations	X	X	X	X	X	X
Properties of operations	X	X	X	X	X	X
Fluency with operations	X	X	X	X	X	X
Using mental math	X	X	X	X	X	X
Estimation						
Selecting appropriate methods						
Data Analysis and Probability						
Represent data using tables and graphs	X	X				
Predicting outcomes	X	X	X	X	X	X
Problem Solving	X	X	X	X	X	X
Reasoning and Proof	X	X	X	X	X	X
Communication		X	X	X	X	X

Sum Dice Graph Activities

Directions for Sum Dice Graph Activities

Objectives:

- Practice computing the sum of number combinations 1 through 12
- Practice multiplication facts 2 through 12
- Recognize and reinforce the sequence of multiples
- Practice directionality on an *x–y* axis

Introduce the Sum Dice Graphs by demonstrating on an overhead.

How to Play

- Toss 2 dice. Find the sum. Multiply the sum by the number specified for that activity.
- Multiples of the number are in sequence on the *x*-axis (bottom row) of the graph.
- Find the multiple and write the multiple in the box above it, or write the number sentence that produced the multiple. For example, for 16 write 2 × 8.

Variations

The student tosses the dice, finds the sum, and multiplies the sum by the number specified on the chart, but instead of recording the product, performs any of the following variations:

- Doubles or triples the multiple
- Halves the multiple
- Adds 5 to the multiple and halves the result

- Adds 7, 8, 9, 10, or 11 to the multiple
- Subtracts 7, 8, 9, 10, 11… (It's possible that a negative number will result!)
- Divides the product by 3 (or any number from 2 to 12)

The student then records that computation in the product column.

Discussion

- When the students have completed their graphs, call attention to the patterns that have emerged.
- Examine the data on many graphs. What columns are more likely to be filled in? Lead students to look at the distribution of sums when tossing 2 dice. (Probability)
- Some students will not notice that the multiples are in sequence on the *x*-axis and will use repeated addition or recall to arrive at the multiplication fact.
- Some students may need to be led to see how to use the information on the graph as a tool.

Dice Activities for Multiplication

2 × Sum Dice Graph

- Toss 2 dice.
- Find the sum.
- Multiply by **2.**
- Fill in the box above the multiple.

4	**6**	**8**	**10**	**12**	**14**	**16**	**18**	**20**	**22**	**24**

3 × Sum Dice Graph

How to Play

- *Toss 2 dice.*
- *Find the sum.*
- *Multiply by **3**.*
- *Fill in the box above the multiple.*

6	9	12	15	18	21	24	27	30	33	36

Dice Activities for Multiplication

4 × Sum Dice Graph

- Toss 2 dice.
- Find the sum.
- Multiply by **4.**
- Fill in the box above the multiple.

					48
					44
					40
					36
					32
					28
					24
					20
					16
					12
					8

5 × Sum Dice Graph

How to Play

- Toss 2 dice.
- Find the sum.
- Multiply by **5.**
- Fill in the box above the multiple.

					60
					55
					50
					45
					40
					35
					30
					25
					20
					15
					10

Dice Activities for Multiplication

6 × Sum Dice Graph

How to Play

- Toss 2 dice.
- Find the sum.
- Multiply by **6.**
- Fill in the box above the multiple.

12	18	24	30	36	42	48	54	60	66	72

7 × Sum Dice Graph

- Toss 2 dice.
- Find the sum.
- Multiply by **7.**
- Fill in the box above the multiple.

14	21	28	35	42	49	56	63	70	77	84

Dice Activities for Multiplication

8 × Sum Dice Graph

- Toss 2 dice.
- Find the sum.
- Multiply by **8**.
- Fill in the box above the multiple.

16	24	32	40	48	56	64	72	80	88	96

Dice Activities for Multiplication

9 × Sum Dice Graph

- Toss 2 dice.
- Find the sum.
- Multiply by **9.**
- Fill in the box above the multiple.

18	27	36	45	54	63	72	81	90	99	108

Dice Activities for Multiplication

10 × Sum Dice Graph

How to Play

- Toss 2 dice.
- Find the sum.
- Multiply by **10**.
- Fill in the box above the multiple.

					120
					110
					100
					90
					80
					70
					60
					50
					40
					30
					20

11 × Sum Dice Graph

- Toss 2 dice.
- Find the sum.
- Multiply by 11.
- Fill in the box above the multiple.

					132
					121
					110
					99
					88
					77
					66
					55
					44
					33
					22

Dice Activities for Multiplication

12 × Sum Dice Graph

How to Play

- Toss 2 dice.
- Find the sum.
- Multiply by **12**.
- Fill in the box above the multiple.

					144
					132
					120
					108
					96
					84
					72
					60
					48
					36
					24

Create Your Own
— × Sum Dice Graph

How to Play

- Choose the number you want to multiply by and write its multiples in the boxes in the bottom row (or see "Variations" on page 2).
- Toss 2 dice. Find the sum.
- Multiply by ___.
- Fill in the box above the multiple.

Table Completion Charts

Contents

Directions for Table Completion Charts

- Practice computing the sum of number combinations 1 through 12
- Practice multiplication facts 2 through 12
- Make the connection that the concept of chance determines who fills in their chart first.

Introduce the Table Completion Charts by demonstrating on an overhead and playing against the class. Two teams with two players on a team are suggested. Teams give students an opportunity to discuss moves and strategies and provide a check on correct computation.

How to Play

Each team tosses a die. The higher number goes first.

- Team tosses two dice, finds the sum, and then multiplies the sum by the number at the top of the chart.
- Records the product next to the sum in the chart.
- If the sum has already been tossed, the team loses a turn.
- First team to complete their chart wins.

Some of the Table Completion activities have two teams play against each other using different multiplicands (for example, 6 vs 7, 6 vs 8, and so on). To play these activities:

- Each team tosses a die and finds the sum.
- Team with the higher number chooses a chart.
- Team with the lower number goes first.

Suggestions

If students are struggling with recalling multiplication facts, suggest that they list the multiples of the multiplicand as a reference.

Before placing a token on the chart, the team members should say the multiplication fact aloud—for example, "Seven times three equals twenty-one."

Variations

The teams toss the dice, find the sum, and multiply by the number on the chart, but instead of recording the product, they perform any of the following variations and record that computation next to the product.

- Double or triple the product.
- Halve the product.
- Add 5 to the product and halve the result.
- Add 7, 8, 9, 10, or 11 to the product.
- Subtract 7, 8, 9, 10, 11… (It's possible to result in a negative number!)
- Tally both columns in each activity and see if there is a pattern.

Discussion

- Is this a game of luck or skill?

Twos Table Completion

- Each team tosses a die.
- Higher number goes first.

How to Play

- Toss 2 dice. Find the sum. Multiply the sum by **2**.
- Record the product next to the sum in the table.
- If the sum has already been tossed, lose a turn.
- First to complete their table wins.

Team: _____

SUM	× 2
12	
11	
10	
9	
8	
7	
6	
5	
4	
3	
2	

Team: _____

SUM	× 2
12	
11	
10	
9	
8	
7	
6	
5	
4	
3	
2	

Threes Table Completion

How to Play

• Toss 2 dice. Find the sum. Multiply the sum by **3**.
• Record the product next to the sum in the table.
• If the sum has already been tossed, lose a turn.
• First to complete their table wins.

Team: _____   Team: _____

SUM	× 3	SUM	× 3
12		12	
11		11	
10		10	
9		9	
8		8	
7		7	
6		6	
5		5	
4		4	
3		3	
2		2	

- Each team tosses a die.
- Higher number goes first.

Fours Table Completion

How to Play

- Toss 2 dice. Find the sum. Multiply the sum by **4.**
- Record the product next to the sum in the table.
- If the sum has already been tossed, lose a turn.
- First to complete their table wins.

Team: _____

SUM	× 4
12	
11	
10	
9	
8	
7	
6	
5	
4	
3	
2	

Team: _____

SUM	× 4
12	
11	
10	
9	
8	
7	
6	
5	
4	
3	
2	

Fives Table Completion

- Each team tosses a die.
- Higher number goes first.

How to Play

- Toss 2 dice. Find the sum. Multiply the sum by **5**.
- Record the product next to the sum in the table.
- If the sum has already been tossed, lose a turn.
- First to complete their table wins.

Team:_____

SUM	× 5
12	
11	
10	
9	
8	
7	
6	
5	
4	
3	
2	

Team:_____

SUM	× 5
12	
11	
10	
9	
8	
7	
6	
5	
4	
3	
2	

- Each team tosses a die.
- Higher number goes first.

How to Play

- Toss 2 dice. Find the sum. Multiply the sum by **6**.
- Record the product next to the sum in the table.
- If the sum has already been tossed, lose a turn.
- First to complete their table wins.

Team: _____

Team: _____

SUM	× 6	SUM	× 6
12		12	
11		11	
10		10	
9		9	
8		8	
7		7	
6		6	
5		5	
4		4	
3		3	
2		2	

- Each team tosses a die.
- Higher number chooses a chart.
- Lower number goes first.

How to Play

- Toss 2 dice. Find the sum. Multiply the sum by the number in the table.
- Record the product next to the sum in the table.
- If the sum has already been tossed, lose a turn.
- First to complete their table wins.

Team: _____   **Team:** _____

SUM	× 6
12	
11	
10	
9	
8	
7	
6	
5	
4	
3	
2	

SUM	× 7
12	
11	
10	
9	
8	
7	
6	
5	
4	
3	
2	

- Each team tosses a die.
- Higher number chooses a chart.
- Lower number goes first.

How to Play

- Toss 2 dice. Find the sum. Multiply the sum by the number in the table.
- Record the product next to the sum in the table.
- If the sum has already been tossed, lose a turn.
- First to complete their table wins.

Team: _____

Team: _____

SUM	× 6	SUM	× 8
12		12	
11		11	
10		10	
9		9	
8		8	
7		7	
6		6	
5		5	
4		4	
3		3	
2		2	

Sevens Table Completion

- Each team tosses a die.
- Higher number goes first.

How to Play

- Toss 2 dice. Find the sum. Multiply the sum by **7**.
- Record the product next to the sum in the table.
- If the sum has already been tossed, lose a turn.
- First to complete their table wins.

Team: _____   **Team:** _____

SUM	× 7	SUM	× 7
12		12	
11		11	
10		10	
9		9	
8		8	
7		7	
6		6	
5		5	
4		4	
3		3	
2		2	

- Each team tosses a die.
- Higher number chooses a chart.
- Lower number goes first.

How to Play

- Toss 2 dice. Find the sum. Multiply the sum by the number in the table.
- Record the product next to the sum in the table.
- If the sum has already been tossed, lose a turn.
- First to complete their table wins.

Team: _____

Team: _____

SUM	× 7
12	
11	
10	
9	
8	
7	
6	
5	
4	
3	
2	

SUM	× 8
12	
11	
10	
9	
8	
7	
6	
5	
4	
3	
2	

- Each team tosses a die.
- Higher number chooses a chart.
- Lower number goes first.

How to Play

- Toss 2 dice. Find the sum. Multiply the sum by the number in the table.
- Record the product next to the sum in the table.
- If the sum has already been tossed, lose a turn.
- First to complete their table wins.

Team: _____

Team: _____

SUM	× 7
12	
11	
10	
9	
8	
7	
6	
5	
4	
3	
2	

SUM	× 9
12	
11	
10	
9	
8	
7	
6	
5	
4	
3	
2	

- Each team tosses a die.
- Higher number goes first.

How to Play

- Toss 2 dice. Find the sum. Multiply the sum by **8.**
- Record the product next to the sum in the table.
- If the sum has already been tossed, lose a turn.
- First to complete their table wins.

Team: _____

Team: _____

SUM	× 8	SUM	× 8
12		12	
11		11	
10		10	
9		9	
8		8	
7		7	
6		6	
5		5	
4		4	
3		3	
2		2	

- Each team tosses a die.
- Higher number chooses a chart.
- Lower number goes first.

How to Play

- Toss 2 dice. Find the sum. Multiply the sum by the number in the table.
- Record the product next to the sum in the table.
- If the sum has already been tossed, lose a turn.
- First to complete their table wins.

Team: _____

Team: _____

SUM	× 8
12	
11	
10	
9	
8	
7	
6	
5	
4	
3	
2	

SUM	× 9
12	
11	
10	
9	
8	
7	
6	
5	
4	
3	
2	

8 vs. 10 Table Completion

- Each team tosses a die.
- Higher number chooses a chart.
- Lower number goes first.

How to Play

- Toss 2 dice. Find the sum. Multiply the sum by the number in the table.
- Record the product next to the sum in the table.
- If the sum has already been tossed, lose a turn.
- First to complete their table wins.

Team: _____   Team: _____

SUM	× 8	SUM	× 10
12		12	
11		11	
10		10	
9		9	
8		8	
7		7	
6		6	
5		5	
4		4	
3		3	
2		2	

Nines Table Completion

- Each team tosses a die.
- Higher number goes first.

How to Play

- Toss 2 dice. Find the sum. Multiply the sum by **9**.
- Record the product next to the sum in the table.
- If the sum has already been tossed, lose a turn.
- First to complete their table wins.

Team: _____

SUM	× 9
12	
11	
10	
9	
8	
7	
6	
5	
4	
3	
2	

Team: _____

SUM	× 9
12	
11	
10	
9	
8	
7	
6	
5	
4	
3	
2	

- Each team tosses a die.
- Higher number chooses a chart.
- Lower number goes first.

How to Play

- Toss 2 dice. Find the sum. Multiply the sum by the number in the table.
- Record the product next to the sum in the table.
- If the sum has already been tossed, lose a turn.
- First to complete their table wins.

Team: _____

SUM	× 9
12	
11	
10	
9	
8	
7	
6	
5	
4	
3	
2	

Team: _____

SUM	× 10
12	
11	
10	
9	
8	
7	
6	
5	
4	
3	
2	

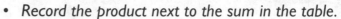

- Each team tosses a die.
- Higher number chooses a chart.
- Lower number goes first.

How to Play

- Toss 2 dice. Find the sum. Multiply the sum by the number in the table.
- Record the product next to the sum in the table.
- If the sum has already been tossed, lose a turn.
- First to complete their table wins.

Team: _____   **Team:** _____

SUM	× 9	SUM	× 11
12		12	
11		11	
10		10	
9		9	
8		8	
7		7	
6		6	
5		5	
4		4	
3		3	
2		2	

Tens Table Completion

- Each team tosses a die.
- Higher number goes first.

How to Play

- Toss 2 dice. Find the sum. Multiply the sum by **10.**
- Record the product next to the sum in the table.
- If the sum has already been tossed, lose a turn.
- First to complete their table wins.

Team: _____

Team: _____

SUM	× 10
12	
11	
10	
9	
8	
7	
6	
5	
4	
3	
2	

SUM	× 10
12	
11	
10	
9	
8	
7	
6	
5	
4	
3	
2	

Elevens Table Completion

How to Play

- *Toss 2 dice. Find the sum. Multiply the sum by 11.*
- *Record the product next to the sum in the table.*
- *If the sum has already been tossed, lose a turn.*
- *First to complete their table wins.*

Team: _____

SUM	× 11
12	
11	
10	
9	
8	
7	
6	
5	
4	
3	
2	

Team: _____

SUM	× 11
12	
11	
10	
9	
8	
7	
6	
5	
4	
3	
2	

Twelves Table Completion

- Each team tosses a die.
- Higher number goes first.

How to Play

- *Toss 2 dice. Find the sum. Multiply the sum by **12**.*
- *Record the product next to the sum in the table.*
- *If the sum has already been tossed, lose a turn.*
- *First to complete their table wins.*

Team: _____

SUM	x 12
12	
11	
10	
9	
8	
7	
6	
5	
4	
3	
2	

Team: _____

SUM	x 12
12	
11	
10	
9	
8	
7	
6	
5	
4	
3	
2	

Create Your Own ___ Table Completion

Each team tosses a die.
Higher number goes first.

How to Play

- Toss 2 dice. Find the sum. Multiply the sum by the number in the table.
- Record the product next to the sum in the table.
- If the sum has already been tossed, lose a turn.
- First to complete their table wins.

Team: _____

SUM	× ___
12	
11	
10	
9	
8	
7	
6	
5	
4	
3	
2	

Team: _____

SUM	× ___
12	
11	
10	
9	
8	
7	
6	
5	
4	
3	
2	

Dice Activities for Multiplication

Four in a Row

Directions for Four in a Row

- Practice computing the sum of number combinations 1 through 12
- Practice multiplication facts 2 through 12
- Develop an awareness of an opponent's possible moves
- Analyze an opponent's possible moves in order to develop a strategy to block opponent
- Distinguish between the role of luck versus skill in an activity using dice
- Develop communication and cooperation skills by working in teams of two students

Introduce the Four in a Row activities by demonstrating on an overhead and playing against the class.

Two teams with two players on a team are suggested. Teams give students an opportunity to discuss moves and strategies and provide a check on correct computation.

How to Play

- Each team tosses a die. The higher number goes first.
- Team tosses two dice, finds the sum, and then multiplies the sum by the specific multiplicand for the activity.
- Team attempts to line up four tokens either vertically, horizontally, or diagonally before the opposing team does.
- First team to align four tokens in a row wins.

Suggestions

If students are struggling with recalling multiplication facts, suggest that they list the multiples of the multiplicand as a reference.

Before placing a token on the chart, the team members should say the multiplication fact aloud—for example, "Seven times three equals twenty-one."

Discussion

- This activity is similar to the games *Othello*® and *Pente*®, where defense is important. How does the toss of the dice influence strategy? Is this activity more a game of defense or offense?
- Does this activity involve more luck or skill?
- Keep a recording of each dice toss. Which combinations were tossed the most? The least?

Four in a Row

Two Dice × 2 Chart

- Two teams with two players on a team.
- Teams toss a die. Higher number goes first.
- Each team chooses a color token.

How to Play

- Toss 2 dice. Find the sum.
- Multiply the sum of the two dice by **2.**
- Place a token on the product.
- First team to get 4 tokens in a row, vertically, horizontally, or diagonally, wins.

18	20	22	10	16	8	14
4	24	14	6	8	14	16
22	18	14	20	20	12	10
10	6	20	16	12	18	12
6	8	12	18	10	14	8
14	22	16	4	12	24	20
16	8	24	10	14	8	6

Four in a Row

Two Dice × 3 Chart

- Two teams with two players on a team.
- Teams toss a die. Higher number goes first.
- Each team chooses a color token.

How to Play

- Toss 2 dice. Find the sum.
- Multiply the sum of the two dice by **3**.
- Place a token on the product.
- First team to get 4 tokens in a row, vertically, horizontally, or diagonally, wins.

27	30	33	15	24	12	18
6	36	21	9	12	21	24
9	27	21	6	30	33	15
15	30	12	21	18	27	18
24	12	18	27	15	21	36
21	33	9	6	18	24	30
24	12	36	15	21	27	9

Four in a Row

Two Dice × 4 Chart

- Two teams with two players on a team.
- Teams toss a die. Higher number goes first.
- Each team chooses a color token.

How to Play

- Toss 2 dice. Find the sum.
- Multiply the sum of the two dice by **4**.
- Place a token on the product.
- First team to get 4 tokens in a row, vertically, horizontally, or diagonally, wins.

28	40	48	20	24	12	16
8	36	32	48	16	28	24
28	44	28	20	8	40	16
20	48	40	24	28	32	36
32	12	44	36	40	8	20
36	32	24	28	16	44	40
20	12	36	16	24	28	32

Four in a Row

Two Dice × 5 Chart

- Two teams with two players on a team.
- Teams toss a die. Higher number goes first.
- Each team chooses a color token.

How to Play

- Toss 2 dice. Find the sum.
- Multiply the sum of the two dice by **5**.
- Place a token on the product.
- First team to get 4 tokens in a row, vertically, horizontally, or diagonally, wins.

35	50	55	25	30	15	20
10	45	40	60	20	45	30
35	50	40	25	10	50	20
20	60	25	30	35	40	45
35	15	55	45	50	35	30
40	10	30	35	20	55	50
25	15	45	25	35	60	40

Dice Activities for Multiplication

Four in a Row

Two Dice × 6 Chart

- Two teams with two players on a team.
- Teams toss a die. Higher number goes first.
- Each team chooses a color token.

How to Play

- Toss 2 dice. Find the sum.
- Multiply the sum of the two dice by **6**.
- Place a token on the product.
- First team to get 4 tokens in a row, vertically, horizontally, or diagonally, wins.

36	60	54	24	66	18	42
12	48	30	72	42	54	36
42	66	48	30	12	60	24
24	72	60	36	42	48	54
30	18	42	54	60	42	30
48	12	36	42	24	66	60
24	18	54	30	36	72	48

Four in a Row

Two Dice × 7 Chart

- Two teams with two players on a team.
- Teams toss a die. Higher number goes first.
- Each team chooses a color token.

How to Play

- Toss 2 dice. Find the sum.
- Multiply the sum of the two dice by **7**.
- Place a token on the product.
- First team to get 4 tokens in a row, vertically, horizontally, or diagonally, wins.

35	70	56	21	63	28	42
14	49	35	63	28	84	56
42	63	49	70	21	49	84
21	77	49	56	42	35	56
70	14	63	35	28	42	77
49	77	28	42	14	63	49
28	35	56	70	49	84	70

Dice Activities for Multiplication

- Two teams with two players on a team.
- Teams toss a die. Higher number goes first.
- Each team chooses a color token.

How to Play

- Toss 2 dice. Find the sum.
- Multiply the sum of the two dice by **8**.
- Place a token on the product.
- First team to get 4 tokens in a row, vertically, horizontally, or diagonally, wins.

32	80	56	24	88	16	80
16	40	80	72	64	56	32
56	88	48	40	72	80	24
24	72	32	64	40	48	56
40	48	64	96	56	72	96
80	32	48	56	64	88	64
96	16	56	40	32	72	48

Four in a Row

Two Dice × 9 Chart

- Two teams with two players on a team.
- Teams toss a die. Higher number goes first.
- Each team chooses a color token.

How to Play

- Toss 2 dice. Find the sum.
- Multiply the sum of the two dice by **9.**
- Place a token on the product.
- First team to get 4 tokens in a row, vertically, horizontally, or diagonally, wins.

81	63	54	27	99	18	45
108	45	90	72	81	54	36
54	63	45	36	72	90	108
18	72	36	63	54	99	81
63	81	63	27	90	72	99
90	36	45	54	81	108	63
27	18	63	90	36	72	45

Four in a Row

Two Dice × 10 Chart

- Two teams with two players on a team.
- Teams toss a die. Higher number goes first.
- Each team chooses a color token.

How to Play

- Toss 2 dice. Find the sum.
- Multiply the sum of the two dice by *10*.
- Place a token on the product.
- First team to get 4 tokens in a row, vertically, horizontally, or diagonally, wins.

100	70	120	50	80	60	30
80	20	90	110	40	100	70
50	90	70	30	90	60	120
40	60	80	100	70	50	80
110	90	50	60	20	70	40
70	40	80	120	60	30	100
20	100	90	70	40	110	50

- Two teams with two players on a team.
- Teams toss a die. Higher number goes first.
- Each team chooses a color token.

How to Play

- Toss 2 dice. Find the sum.
- Multiply the sum of the two dice by 11.
- Place a token on the product.
- First team to get 4 tokens in a row, vertically, horizontally, or diagonally, wins.

110	77	132	55	88	66	33
88	22	99	121	44	110	77
55	99	77	33	99	66	132
44	66	88	110	77	55	88
121	99	55	66	22	77	44
77	44	88	132	66	33	110
22	110	99	77	44	121	55

- Two teams with two players on a team.
- Teams toss a die. Higher number goes first.
- Each team chooses a color token.

How to Play

- Toss 2 dice. Find the sum.
- Multiply the sum of the two dice by 12.
- Place a token on the product.
- First team to get 4 tokens in a row, vertically, horizontally, or diagonally, wins.

120	84	144	60	96	72	36
96	24	108	132	48	120	84
60	108	84	36	108	72	144
48	72	96	120	84	60	96
132	108	60	72	24	84	48
84	48	96	144	72	36	120
24	120	108	84	48	132	60

Square Off

Directions for Square Off

- Practice computing the sum of number combinations 1 through 12
- Practice multiplication facts 2 through 12
- Develop an awareness of an opponent's possible moves
- Analyze an opponent's possible moves in order to develop a strategy to block opponent
- Distinguish between the role of luck versus skill in an activity using dice
- Develop communication and cooperation skills by working in teams of two students

Introduce **Square Off** by demonstrating on an overhead and playing against the class.

Two teams with two players on a team are suggested. Teams give students an opportunity to discuss moves and strategies and provide a check on correct computation.

How to Play

- Each team tosses a die. The higher number goes first.

- Teams toss two dice, find the sum, and multiply the sum by the specific multiplicand for the activity.

- Teams attempt to arrange four tokens to form any size square, 2-by-2, 3-by-3, 4-by-4, and so on. Orientation of the square can be on the diagonal.

- First team to form three squares wins.

Suggestions

If students are struggling with recalling multiplication facts, suggest that they list the multiples of the multiplicand as a reference.

Before placing a token on the chart, the team members should say the multiplication fact aloud—for example, "Seven times three equals twenty-one."

Discussion

- Is this more a game of luck or skill?

- Is there more opportunity in **Square Off** than in **Four in a Row** or **Cross Over** to play defensively—that is, to prevent the opposing team from making a square?

- Which of the three activities, **Square Off**, **Four in a Row**, or **Cross Over**, offers more opportunities to block the other team? Why is that?

Square Off

Two Dice × 2 Chart

- Each team chooses a color token.
- Toss a die.
- Higher number goes first.

How to Play

- Toss 2 dice. Find the sum.
- Multiply the sum of the two dice by **2**.
- Place a token on the product.
- If the product has a token on it, lose a turn.
- First team to place tokens forming three squares wins.

18	20	22	10	16	8	14
4	24	14	6	8	14	16
22	18	14	20	20	12	10
10	6	20	16	12	18	12
6	8	12	18	10	14	8
14	22	16	4	12	24	20
16	8	24	10	14	18	6

Square Off

Two Dice × 3 Chart

- Each team chooses a color token.
- Toss a die.
- Higher number goes first.

How to Play

- Toss 2 dice. Find the sum.
- Multiply the sum of the two dice by **3**.
- Place a token on the product.
- If the product has a token on it, lose a turn.
- First team to place tokens forming three squares wins.

27	30	33	15	24	12	18
6	36	21	9	12	21	24
9	27	21	6	30	33	15
15	30	12	21	18	27	18
24	12	18	27	15	21	36
21	33	9	6	18	24	30
24	12	36	15	21	27	9

Square Off

Two Dice × 4 Chart

- Each team chooses a color token.
- Toss a die.
- Higher number goes first.

How to Play

- Toss 2 dice. Find the sum.
- Multiply the sum of the two dice by **4**.
- Place a token on the product.
- If the product has a token on it, lose a turn.
- First team to place tokens forming three squares wins.

28	40	48	20	24	12	16
8	36	32	48	16	28	24
28	44	28	20	8	40	16
20	48	40	24	28	32	36
32	12	44	36	40	8	20
36	32	24	28	16	44	40
20	12	36	16	24	28	32

Square Off

Two Dice × 5 Chart

- Each team chooses a color token.
- Toss a die.
- Higher number goes first.

How to Play

- Toss 2 dice. Find the sum.
- *Multiply the sum of the two dice by 5.*
- *Place a token on the product.*
- *If the product has a token on it, lose a turn.*
- *First team to place tokens forming three squares wins.*

35	50	55	25	30	15	20
10	45	40	60	20	45	30
35	50	40	25	10	50	20
20	60	25	30	35	40	45
35	15	55	45	50	35	30
40	10	30	35	20	55	50
25	15	45	25	35	60	40

- Each team chooses a color token.
- Toss a die.
- Higher number goes first.

How to Play

- Toss 2 dice. Find the sum.
- *Multiply the sum of the two dice by* **6.**
- *Place a token on the product.*
- *If the product has a token on it, lose a turn.*
- *First team to place tokens forming three squares wins.*

36	60	54	24	66	18	42
12	48	30	72	42	54	36
42	66	48	30	12	60	24
24	72	60	36	42	48	54
30	18	42	54	60	42	30
48	12	36	42	24	66	60
24	18	54	30	36	72	48

Square Off

Two Dice × 7 Chart

- Each team chooses a color token.
- Toss a die.
- Higher number goes first.

How to Play

- Toss 2 dice. Find the sum.
- Multiply the sum of the two dice by **7**.
- Place a token on the product.
- If the product has a token on it, lose a turn.
- First team to place tokens forming three squares wins.

35	70	56	21	63	28	42
14	49	35	63	28	84	56
42	63	49	70	21	49	84
21	77	49	56	42	35	56
70	14	63	35	28	42	77
49	77	28	42	14	63	49
28	35	56	70	49	84	70

Dice Activities for Multiplication © Didax — www.didax.com

Square Off

Two Dice × 8 Chart

- Each team chooses a color token.
- Toss a die.
- Higher number goes first.

How to Play

- Toss 2 dice. *Find the sum.*
- *Multiply the sum of the two dice by **8**.*
- *Place a token on the product.*
- *If the product has a token on it, lose a turn.*
- *First team to place tokens forming three squares wins.*

32	80	56	24	88	16	80
16	40	80	72	64	56	32
56	88	48	40	72	80	24
24	72	32	64	40	48	56
40	48	64	96	56	72	96
80	32	48	56	64	88	64
96	16	56	40	32	72	48

- Each team chooses a color token.
- Toss a die.
- Higher number goes first.

How to Play

- Toss 2 dice. Find the sum.
- Multiply the sum of the two dice by **9**.
- Place a token on the product.
- If the product has a token on it, lose a turn.
- First team to place tokens forming three squares wins.

81	63	54	27	99	18	45
108	45	90	72	81	54	36
54	63	45	36	72	90	108
18	72	36	63	54	99	81
63	81	63	27	90	72	99
90	36	45	54	81	108	63
27	18	63	90	36	72	45

- Each team chooses a color token.
- Toss a die.
- Higher number goes first.

How to Play

- Toss 2 dice. Find the sum.
- Multiply the sum of the two dice by **10**.
- Place a token on the product.
- If the product has a token on it, lose a turn.
- First team to place tokens forming three squares wins.

100	70	120	50	80	60	30
80	20	90	110	40	100	70
50	90	70	30	90	60	120
40	60	80	100	70	50	80
110	90	50	60	20	70	40
70	40	80	120	60	30	100
20	100	90	70	40	110	50

Square Off

Two Dice × 11 Chart

- Each team chooses a color token.
- Toss a die.
- Higher number goes first.

How to Play

- Toss 2 dice. Find the sum.
- Multiply the sum of the two dice by 11.
- Place a token on the product.
- If the product has a token on it, lose a turn.
- First team to place tokens forming three squares wins.

110	77	132	55	88	66	33
88	22	99	121	44	110	77
55	99	77	33	99	66	132
44	66	88	110	77	55	88
121	99	55	66	22	77	44
77	44	88	132	66	33	110
22	110	99	77	44	121	55

Two Dice × 12 Chart

- Each team chooses a color token.
- Toss a die.
- Higher number goes first.

How to Play

- Toss 2 dice. Find the sum.
- Multiply the sum of the two dice by 12.
- Place a token on the product.
- If the product has a token on it, lose a turn.
- First team to place tokens forming three squares wins.

120	84	144	60	96	72	36
96	24	108	132	48	120	84
60	108	84	36	108	72	144
48	72	96	120	84	60	96
132	108	60	72	24	84	48
84	48	96	144	72	36	120
24	120	108	84	48	132	60

Cross Over

Directions for Cross Over

- Practice computing the sum of number combinations 1 through 12
- Practice multiplication facts 2 through 12
- Develop an awareness of an opponent's possible moves
- Analyze an opponent's possible moves in order to develop a strategy to block opponent
- Distinguish between the role of luck versus skill in an activity using dice
- Develop communication and cooperation skills by working in teams of two students

Introduce **Cross Over** by demonstrating on an overhead and playing against the class. The goal is to be the first team to make a connected line of tokens across the board.

Two teams with two players on a team are suggested.

How to Play

- Each team tosses a die. Team with the higher number goes first.

- Team A tosses two dice, finds the sum, and multiplies the sum by the specific multiplicand for the activity.

- Team A locates the product in either the outside right or outside left column of the chart and places a token on the product. If no box in either column contains the product, the team loses its turn.

- Team B tosses two dice, finds the sum, and multiplies the sum by the specific multiplicand for the activity. The team must place its first token in the outside column on the opposite side of the chart from Team A's first token.

- With each toss of the dice, the teams attempt to place their tokens in continuous alignment, connecting them vertically, horizontally, or diagonally to reach the opposite side of the chart. The path across the chart may meander on its way to the other side.

- First team to reach the opposite side wins.

Suggestions

If students are struggling with recalling multiplication facts, suggest that they list the multiples of the multiplicand as a reference.

Before placing a token on the chart, the team members should say the multiplication fact aloud—for example, "Seven times three equals twenty-one."

Discussion

- Is this more a game of luck or skill?

- Which of the three activities, **Square Off**, **Four in a Row**, or **Cross Over**, offers more opportunities to block the other team? Why?

Cross Over

Two Dice × 2 Chart

- Two teams with two players on a team.
- Teams toss a die. Higher number goes first.
- Each team chooses a color token.
- Teams start on opposite sides of the chart.

How to Play

- Toss 2 dice. Find the sum.
- Multiply the sum by **2.** Place a token on the product.
- If the product has a token on it, lose a turn.
- First to cross over wins.

18	20	22	10	16	8	14
4	24	14	6	8	14	16
22	18	14	20	20	12	10
10	6	20	16	12	18	12
6	8	12	18	10	14	8
14	22	16	4	12	24	20
16	8	24	10	14	18	6

Cross Over

Two Dice × 3 Chart

- Two teams with two players on a team.
- Teams toss a die. Higher number goes first.
- Each team chooses a color token.
- Teams start on opposite sides of the chart.

How to Play

- Toss 2 dice. Find the sum.
- Multiply the sum by **3.** Place a token on the product.
- If the product has a token on it, lose a turn.
- First to cross over wins.

27	30	33	15	24	12	18
6	36	21	9	12	21	24
9	27	21	6	30	33	15
15	30	12	21	18	27	18
24	12	18	27	15	21	36
21	33	9	6	18	24	30
24	12	36	15	21	27	9

Dice Activities for Multiplication

Cross Over

Two Dice × 4 Chart

- Two teams with two players on a team.
- Teams toss a die. Higher number goes first.
- Each team chooses a color token.
- Teams start on opposite sides of the chart.

How to Play

- Toss 2 dice. Find the sum.
- Multiply the sum by **4.** Place a token on the product.
- If the product has a token on it, lose a turn.
- First to cross over wins.

28	40	48	20	24	12	16
8	36	32	48	16	28	24
28	44	28	20	8	40	16
20	48	40	24	28	32	36
32	12	44	36	40	8	20
36	32	24	28	16	44	40
20	12	36	16	24	28	32

Cross Over

Two Dice × 5 Chart

- Two teams with two players on a team.
- Teams toss a die. Higher number goes first.
- Each team chooses a color token.
- Teams start on opposite sides of the chart.

How to Play

- *Toss 2 dice. Find the sum.*
- *Multiply the sum by **5**. Place a token on the product.*
- *If the product has a token on it, lose a turn.*
- *First to cross over wins.*

35	50	55	25	30	15	20
10	45	40	60	20	45	30
35	50	40	25	10	50	20
20	60	25	30	35	40	45
35	15	55	45	50	35	30
40	10	30	35	20	55	50
25	15	45	25	35	60	40

Dice Activities for Multiplication

Cross Over

Two Dice × 6 Chart

- Two teams with two players on a team.
- Teams toss a die. Higher number goes first.
- Each team chooses a color token.
- Teams start on opposite sides of the chart.

How to Play

- *Toss 2 dice. Find the sum.*
- *Multiply the sum by **6**. Place a token on the product.*
- *If the product has a token on it, lose a turn.*
- *First to cross over wins.*

36	60	54	24	66	18	42
12	48	30	72	42	54	36
42	66	48	30	12	60	24
24	72	60	36	42	48	54
30	18	42	54	60	42	30
48	12	36	42	24	66	60
24	18	54	30	36	72	48

Cross Over

Two Dice × 7 Chart

- Two teams with two players on a team.
- Teams toss a die. Higher number goes first.
- Each team chooses a color token.
- Teams start on opposite sides of the chart.

How to Play

- Toss 2 dice. Find the sum.
- Multiply the sum by **7**. Place a token on the product.
- If the product has a token on it, lose a turn.
- First to cross over wins.

35	70	56	21	63	28	42
14	49	35	63	28	84	56
42	63	49	70	21	49	84
21	77	49	56	42	35	56
70	14	63	35	28	42	77
49	77	28	42	14	63	49
28	35	56	70	49	84	70

Dice Activities for Multiplication

Cross Over

Two Dice × 8 Chart

- Two teams with two players on a team.
- Teams toss a die. Higher number goes first.
- Each team chooses a color token.
- Teams start on opposite sides of the chart.

How to Play

- *Toss 2 dice. Find the sum.*
- *Multiply the sum by **8**. Place a token on the product.*
- *If the product has a token on it, lose a turn.*
- *First to cross over wins.*

32	80	56	24	88	16	80
16	40	80	72	64	56	32
56	88	48	40	72	80	24
24	72	32	64	40	48	56
40	48	64	96	56	72	96
80	32	48	56	64	88	64
96	16	56	40	32	72	48

Cross Over

Two Dice × 9 Chart

- Two teams with two players on a team.
- Teams toss a die. Higher number goes first.
- Each team chooses a color token.
- Teams start on opposite sides of the chart.

How to Play

- Toss 2 dice. Find the sum.
- Multiply the sum by **9.** Place a token on the product.
- If the product has a token on it, lose a turn.
- First to cross over wins.

81	63	54	27	99	18	45
108	45	90	72	81	54	36
54	63	45	36	72	90	108
18	72	36	63	54	99	81
63	81	63	27	90	72	99
90	36	45	54	81	108	63
27	18	63	90	36	72	45

Cross Over

- Two teams with two players on a team.
- Teams toss a die. Higher number goes first.
- Each team chooses a color token.
- Teams start on opposite sides of the chart.

How to Play

- Toss 2 dice. Find the sum.
- Multiply the sum by **10**. Place a token on the product.
- If the product has a token on it, lose a turn.
- First to cross over wins.

100	70	120	50	80	60	30
80	20	90	110	40	100	70
50	90	70	30	90	60	120
40	60	80	100	70	50	80
110	90	50	60	20	70	40
70	40	80	120	60	30	100
20	100	90	70	40	110	50

Cross Over

Two Dice × 11 Chart

- Two teams with two players on a team.
- Teams toss a die. Higher number goes first.
- Each team chooses a color token.
- Teams start on opposite sides of the chart.

How to Play

- *Toss 2 dice. Find the sum.*
- *Multiply the sum by 11. Place a token on the product.*
- *If the product has a token on it, lose a turn.*
- *First to cross over wins.*

110	77	132	55	88	66	33
88	22	99	121	44	110	77
55	99	77	33	99	66	132
44	66	88	110	77	55	88
121	99	55	66	22	77	44
77	44	88	132	66	33	110
22	110	99	77	44	121	55

Cross Over

Two Dice × 12 Chart

- Two teams with two players on a team.
- Teams toss a die. Higher number goes first.
- Each team chooses a color token.
- Teams start on opposite sides of the chart.

How to Play

- *Toss 2 dice. Find the sum.*
- *Multiply the sum by 12. Place a token on the product.*
- *If the product has a token on it, lose a turn.*
- *First to cross over wins.*

120	84	144	60	96	72	36
96	24	108	132	48	120	84
60	108	84	36	108	72	144
48	72	96	120	84	60	96
132	108	60	72	24	84	48
84	48	96	144	72	36	120
24	120	108	84	48	132	60

Tic-Tac-Toe / Four-Grid Tic-Tac-Toe

Contents

Objectives:

- Practice computing the sum of number combinations 1 through 12

- Practice multiplication facts 2 through 12

- Develop an understanding of the difference between a "fair game" and a "game of chance"

- Develop communication and cooperation skills by working in teams of two students

The Tic-Tac-Toe activities introduce the standard game of Tic-Tac-Toe and introduce students to the concepts of fair chance and what makes a game fair.

Each Tic-Tac-Toe activity is paired with a Four-Grid Tic-Tac-Toe activity, providing a way to diversify reinforcing multiplication facts. This presents opportunities for students to practice playing Tic-Tac-Toe with each set of multiples 2 through 9, before moving on to the more complicated Four-Grid Tic-Tac-Toe.

Warm-Up Activity: Tic-Tac Toe

Introduce the Tic-Tac-Toe activities by demonstrating a standard game of Tic-Tac-Toe, using Xs and Os and playing against the class.

- Decide who is to use X and who is to use O.

- Each side tosses a die. Higher number goes first.

- Players take turns placing their X or O on the 3-by-3 Tic-Tac-Toe grid.

- First side to place three Xs or Os in continuous alignment, vertically, horizontally, or diagonally, wins the game.

- First side to win 2 out of 3 games is the winner.

Discussion

- Does the person who goes first have an advantage?

- Is this a game of luck or skill?

- Is it a fair game?

How to Play:
Two-Dice × 2 Tic-Tac-Toe

- Introduce the **Two-Dice × 2 Tic-Tac-Toe** activity by demonstrating it on an overhead and playing against the class.

- Two players on a team are suggested. Teams give students an opportunity to discuss moves and strategies and provide a check on correct computation.

- Each team chooses a color token and tosses a die. Higher number goes first.

- Team tosses two dice, finds the sum, and then multiplies the sum by the multiplicand for the activity (in this activity, 2).

- Team places a token on the product on the Tic-Tac-Toe grid.

- With each dice toss, teams attempt to place their tokens in continuous alignment, vertically, horizontally, or diagonally, to win the game.

- If the product is not shown on the grid or already has a token on it, team loses a turn.

- First team to form a Tic-Tac-Toe vertically, horizontally, or diagonally wins.

- Teams play 3 games.

- Team winning 2 out of 3 games is the winner.

Discussion

- How does the dice toss influence your strategy?

- How does the dice toss influence the outcome of the game?

- Is there a fair chance of each multiple being tossed?

- Is this a fair game?

Suggestions

If students are struggling with recalling multiplication facts, suggest that they list the multiples of the multiplicand as a reference.

Before placing a token on the chart, the team members should say the multiplication fact aloud—for example, "Seven times three equals twenty-one."

How to Play:
Two Dice × 2 Four-Grid Tic-Tac-Toe

- Introduce **Two Dice × 2 Four-Grid Tic-Tac-Toe** by demonstrating on an overhead and playing against the class.

- Each team chooses a color token and tosses a die. Higher number goes first.

- The team tosses two dice, finds the sum, and then multiplies the sum by the specific multiplicand for the activity (in this case, 2).

- The team locates the product on any of the Tic-Tac-Toe grids and places a token on *only one* of the products.

- With each dice toss, teams attempt to place their tokens in continuous alignment, vertically, horizontally, or diagonally, forming as many Tic-Tac-Toe wins as possible.

- If a product is not shown on the grid or already has a token on it, the team loses a turn.

- When no more plays are possible, teams count their Tic-Tac-Toe wins. The team with more Tic-Tac-Toes wins.

Variation:

- The team tosses two dice, finds the sum, and multiples the sum by the multiplicand for the activity.

- The team places a token in *every* box where that product appears on all four Tic-Tac-Toe grids.

Discussion

- Is this a game of luck or skill?

- Is there opportunity to play defensively?

- What are the most Tic-Tac-Toe wins possible on one of the grids?

- Which strategy works best: trying to get the most three tokens in a row or trying to block your opponent?

Agree with your opponents to both use the same strategy to see what happens. Agree to each use a different strategy.

Dice Activities for Multiplication

Two Dice × 2 Tic-Tac-Toe

How to Play

- Toss 2 dice. Find the sum.
- Multiply the sum by **2**.
- Find the product on the grid and place a token on it.
- If number already has a token on it, lose a turn.
- First team to get three in a row wins.
- Play 3 games. Team winning 2 out of 3 games wins.

8	6	16
14	18	22
10	12	20

Dice Activities for Multiplication

Two Dice × 2

Four-Grid Tic-Tac-Toe

- Each team chooses a color token.
- Toss die. Higher number goes first.

- Toss 2 dice. Find the sum.
- Multiply the sum by **2**.
- Find the product on **one** of the 4 Tic-Tac-Toe grids and place a token on it.
- If the number is not available on any grid, lose a turn.
- Team with the most threes in a row wins.

4	20	10	6	22	12
22	14	8	14	16	10
18	12	24	18	8	40
12	14	16	8	18	10
20	18	8	20	24	22
22	10	6	14	16	6

- Each team chooses a color token.
- Toss die. Higher number goes first.

How to Play

- Toss 2 dice. Find the sum.
- Multiply the sum by **3**.
- Find the product on the grid and place a token on it.
- If number already has a token on it, lose a turn.
- First team to get three in a row wins.
- Play 3 games. Team winning 2 out of 3 games wins.

12	**9**	**24**
21	**27**	**33**
15	**18**	**30**

Two Dice × 3

Four-Grid Tic-Tac-Toe

- Each team chooses a color token.
- Toss die. Higher number goes first.

How to Play

- Toss 2 dice. Find the sum.
- Multiply the sum by **3**.
- Find the product on **one** of the 4 Tic-Tac-Toe grids and place a token on it.
- If the number is not available on any grid, lose a turn.
- Team with the most "threes in a row" wins.

6	30	12	15	33	9
27	21	15	21	18	12
24	18	36	27	30	24
15	21	24	30	27	21
30	27	18	12	24	33
21	12	9	21	15	18

- Each team chooses a color token.
- Toss die. Higher number goes first.

How to Play

- Toss 2 dice. Find the sum.
- Multiply the sum by **4.**
- Find the product on the grid and place a token on it.
- If number already has a token on it, lose a turn.
- First team to get three in a row wins.
- Play 3 games. Team winning 2 out of 3 games wins.

12	**36**	**32**
24	**28**	**44**
16	**20**	**40**

Two Dice × 4

Four-Grid Tic-Tac-Toe

- Each team chooses a color token.
- Toss die. Higher number goes first.

How to Play

- *Toss 2 dice. Find the sum.*
- *Multiply the sum by **4**.*
- *Find the product on **one** of the 4 Tic-Tac-Toe grids and place a token on it.*
- *If the number is not available on any grid, lose a turn.*
- *Team with the most threes in a row wins.*

8	40	20	12	44	24
44	28	16	28	32	20
36	24	48	36	16	40
24	28	32	16	36	20
40	36	16	40	24	44
44	20	12	28	32	12

- Each team chooses a color token.
- Toss die. Higher number goes first.

How to Play

- Toss 2 dice. Find the sum.
- Multiply the sum by **5.**
- Find the product on the grid and place a token on it.
- If number already has a token on it, lose a turn.
- First team to get three in a row wins.
- Play 3 games. Team winning 2 out of 3 games wins.

45	**35**	**15**
30	**25**	**55**
50	**20**	**40**

Two Dice × 5

Four-Grid Tic-Tac-Toe

- Each team chooses a color token.
- Toss die. Higher number goes first.

How to Play

- *Toss 2 dice. Find the sum.*
- *Multiply the sum by **5**.*
- *Find the product on **one** of the 4 Tic-Tac-Toe grids and place a token on it.*
- *If the number is not available on any grid, lose a turn.*
- *Team with the most threes in a row wins.*

10	50	20	15	55	25
55	35	15	35	30	20
40	25	60	45	50	40
25	35	40	30	45	20
50	45	30	50	40	55
55	20	15	35	25	15

- Each team chooses a color token.
- Toss die. Higher number goes first.

How to Play

- Toss 2 dice. Find the sum.
- Multiply the sum by **6**.
- Find the product on the grid and place a token on it.
- If number already has a token on it, lose a turn.
- First team to get three in a row wins.
- Play 3 games. Team winning 2 out of 3 games wins.

54	**42**	**18**
36	**30**	**66**
60	**24**	**48**

Two Dice × 6

Four-Grid Tic-Tac-Toe

How to Play

- Toss 2 dice. Find the sum.
- Multiply the sum by **6**.
- Find the product on **one** of the 4 Tic-Tac-Toe grids and place a token on it.
- If the number is not available on any grid, lose a turn.
- Team with the most threes in a row wins.

12	60	24	18	66	30
66	42	18	42	36	24
48	30	72	54	60	48
30	42	48	36	54	30
60	54	36	60	48	66
36	42	54	42	24	18

- Each team chooses a color token.
- Toss die. Higher number goes first.

How to Play

- Toss 2 dice. Find the sum.
- Multiply the sum by **7**.
- Find the product on the grid and place a token on it.
- If number already has a token on it, lose a turn.
- First team to get three in a row wins.
- Play 3 games. Team winning 2 out of 3 games wins.

56	**42**	**21**
28	**35**	**77**
70	**49**	**63**

Dice Activities for Multiplication

Two Dice × 7

Four-Grid Tic-Tac-Toe

- Each team chooses a color token.
- Toss die. Higher number goes first.

How to Play

- Toss 2 dice. Find the sum.
- Multiply the sum by **7**.
- Find the product on **one** of the 4 Tic-Tac-Toe grids and place a token on it.
- If the number is not available on any grid, lose a turn.
- Team with the most threes in a row wins.

14	70	28	21	77	35
77	42	21	42	49	28
49	35	84	56	63	70
70	42	49	35	56	70
63	56	35	77	63	21
21	28	14	42	49	28

- Each team chooses a color token.
- Toss die. Higher number goes first.

How to Play

- Toss 2 dice. Find the sum.
- Multiply the sum by **8**.
- Find the product on the grid and place a token on it.
- If number already has a token on it, lose a turn.
- First team to get three in a row wins.
- Play 3 games. Team winning 2 out of 3 games wins.

56	48	64
32	40	88
80	24	72

Two Dice × 8

Four-Grid Tic-Tac-Toe

- Each team chooses a color token.
- Toss die. Higher number goes first.

How to Play

- Toss 2 dice. Find the sum.
- Multiply the sum by **8**.
- Find the product on **one** of the 4 Tic-Tac-Toe grids and place a token on it.
- If the number is not available on any grid, lose a turn.
- Team with the most threes in a row wins.

16	80	72	88	56	40
88	48	56	72	32	64
32	40	64	56	80	48
72	32	48	56	64	96
80	64	42	40	48	80
24	40	56	32	24	72

Two Dice × 9 Tic-Tac-Toe

- Each team chooses a color token.
- Toss die. Higher number goes first.

How to Play

- Toss 2 dice. Find the sum.
- Multiply the sum by **9**.
- Find the product on the grid and place a token on it.
- If number already has a token on it, lose a turn.
- First team to get three in a row wins.
- Play 3 games. Team winning 2 out of 3 games wins.

54	**45**	**63**
36	**81**	**99**
90	**27**	**72**

Dice Activities for Multiplication © Didax – www.didax.com

Two Dice × 9

- Each team chooses a color token.
- Toss die. Higher number goes first.

How to Play

- Toss 2 dice. Find the sum.
- Multiply the sum by **9**.
- Find the product on **one** of the 4 Tic-Tac-Toe grids and place a token on it.
- If the number is not available on any grid, lose a turn.
- Team with the most threes in a row wins.

18	90	81	99	63	45
99	54	63	81	36	72
36	45	72	108	90	54
81	36	54	36	72	99
90	72	63	45	63	90
27	45	99	81	27	54

- Each team chooses a color token.
- Toss die. Higher number goes first.

How to Play

- *Toss 2 dice. Find the sum.*
- *Multiply the sum by 10.*
- *Find the product on the grid and place a token on it.*
- *If number already has a token on it, lose a turn.*
- *First team to get three in a row wins.*
- *Play 3 games. Team winning 2 out of 3 games wins.*

50	**60**	**90**
80	**70**	**110**
100	**30**	**40**

Two Dice × 10

Four-Grid Tic-Tac-Toe

- Each team chooses a color token.
- Toss die. Higher number goes first.

How to Play

- Toss 2 dice. Find the sum.
- Multiply the sum by **10**.
- Find the product on **one** of the 4 Tic-Tac-Toe grids and place a token on it.
- If the number is not available on any grid, lose a turn.
- Team with the most threes in a row wins.

20	100	40	30	90	50
110	70	60	70	60	40
80	50	120	90	100	80
50	70	80	60	90	40
100	90	60	100	80	70
110	40	70	70	50	30

Two Dice × 11 Tic-Tac-Toe

How to Play

- Toss 2 dice. Find the sum.
- Multiply the sum by 11.
- Find the product on the grid and place a token on it.
- If number already has a token on it, lose a turn.
- First team to get three in a row wins.
- Play 3 games. Team winning 2 out of 3 games wins.

33	**99**	**88**
66	**77**	**121**
44	**55**	**110**

Two Dice × 11

Four-Grid Tic-Tac-Toe

- Each team chooses a color token.
- Toss die. Higher number goes first.

How to Play

- *Toss 2 dice. Find the sum.*
- *Multiply the sum by **11**.*
- *Find the product on **one** of the 4 Tic-Tac-Toe grids and place a token on it.*
- *If the number is not available on any grid, lose a turn.*
- *Team with the most threes in a row wins.*

22	110	44	33	121	55
99	77	66	77	66	44
88	55	132	99	110	88
55	77	88	66	99	44
110	99	66	110	88	77
121	44	77	77	55	33

- Each team chooses a color token.
- Toss die. Higher number goes first.

How to Play

- *Toss dice. Find the sum.*
- *Multiply the sum by 12.*
- *Find the product on the grid and place a token on it.*
- *If number already has a token on it, lose a turn.*
- *First team to get three in a row wins.*
- *Play 3 games. Team winning 2 out of 3 games wins.*

132	**108**	**96**
84	**72**	**36**
48	**60**	**120**

Dice Activities for Multiplication © Didax – www.didax.com

Two Dice × 12

Four-Grid Tic-Tac-Toe

- Each team chooses a color token.
- Toss die. Higher number goes first.

How to Play

- *Toss 2 dice. Find the sum.*
- *Multiply the sum by **12**.*
- *Find the product on **one** of the 4 Tic-Tac-Toe grids and place a token on it.*
- *If the number is not available on any grid, lose a turn.*
- *Team with the most threes in a row wins.*

24	120	48	36	132	60
108	84	72	84	72	48
96	60	144	108	120	96
60	84	96	72	108	48
120	108	72	120	96	84
132	48	84	84	60	36

The Math of Course group members met while teaching at the Josiah Haynes Elementary School in Sudbury, Massachusetts. They continue their journey together as staff developers in public school districts throughout New England.

Chet Delani holds a doctorate from Boston College and a master's degree in mathematics education from Boston University. A nationally recognized trainer of teachers in grades K–8 mathematics, he is currently on the faculty of Cambridge College, Cambridge, Massachusetts. His work with classroom teachers is supported by 39 years as a classroom teacher and elementary school principal.

Mary Holt Saltus earned a CAS degree in human development from Harvard Graduate School of Education and a master's degree from Wheelock College. As a Peace Corps volunteer, she was a teacher trainer for the Van Leer Foundation for Early Childhood Education. Currently she is researching the links between understanding math concepts and reading comprehension.

Diane Phelps Neison earned an M.Ed. from Lesley University (formerly Lesley College) and a B.A. in English from Rider University (Lawrenceville, New Jersey). She began her teaching career in New York and New Jersey schools, and has taught at the Haynes School for 26 years.

Karen Kane Moore holds an M.S. in early childhood education from Wheelock College. She is the founder of MathYes, an after-school math enrichment program.

Marcia Roak Fitzgerald received a B.A. in elementary education from the University of Maine. During her 30 years as a classroom teacher at the Haynes School, she has used a multi-manipulative approach to teaching math.

The Math of Course group thanks their agent John Baack and the staff of the Josiah Haynes School for their continued support.

Also by the same authors: *Dice Activities for Math,* a collection of one-, two-, and three-dice activities to develop fluency in addition, subtraction, halving, and place value in children in grades K–3. Available from Didax (www.didax.com / 800-458-0024).

Double the Die Plus
One Chart

- Each player chooses a color token (tiles, cubes, chips).
- Players toss die. Highest number goes first.

How to Play

- Toss die.
- Double the amount.
- Add one.
- Find the number on the chart.
- Place one token on the number.
- If number has a token on it, lose a turn.
- Count tokens to see who wins.

13	3	7	9	5
11	13	9	7	11
9	11	7	3	5
3	13	3	11	13
7	9	5	9	7
5	3	11	13	3